Islander

Islander

Lynn Davidson

Victoria University Press

VICTORIA UNIVERSITY PRESS
Victoria University of Wellington
PO Box 600 Wellington
vup.victoria.ac.nz

Published simultaneously in the United Kingdom by Shearsman Books

ISBN 9781776562350

A catalogue record is available at the National Library of New Zealand

Printed by Ligare

ACKNOWLEDGEMENTS

Thanks to the editors of the following publications in which some of
the poems have appeared: *Sport, PN Review, Australian Poetry Journal,
4th Floor, Kiss Me Hardy, New Writing Scotland, Boast* and
Another English: Anglophone Poems from Around the World

Some of the poems were written as part of my PhD at Massey University. Thanks
to Ingrid Horrocks and Bryan Walpert for guidance and a good eye

I am very grateful for a Hawthornden Castle Fellowship and a
Bothy Project Residency, both of which helped me to write this collection

Many thanks to my wonderful companion writers in 12

For Elliot and Tamara, with love

Contents

Return to Islay

Standing Places

Bass Rock

Light

My stair

Between the sea and my window
the bus depot where
late at night, double decker buses all
empty and delicate and full of light

glide in, pausing over concrete gullies
where little arms reach up to touch
their underneaths where movement starts.
My father's heart is failing, he fills up

with fluid (like an empty bus fills up with light?)
I look for flights.
I live on the second floor of the stair.
More Gunn Furness Gray. I am

a lodger here, where buses lightly lumber
into the yellow depot
like bubbles back
into solution.

Leaving Bass Rock gannet colony

After skypointing to show
it's ready

after one last dive, shorting the sea
(the crack, the pressured current fizzing)

after one last moment of great aloneness: a fleck
in oceans

after the last fish in its gut –
the fin and skin and bone of it – tears apart

it takes a final flight, blowing
Bass Rock into the feathery pieces   we call

aura or
atoms   we called

father or
Adam

Ancient light

makes the space in which vision
is possible.

Ancient light

inscribed on the side of a house
gives warning against
the obstruction of light.

Ancient light

finds the opening in the wall
for the admission of light.

Ancient light

from the first voyage, the first great aloneness,
falls in shaking ribbons on the cars.

In their light

we call our hunting and foraging mothers and fathers
our first ancients, our dear ones,
in from the hills. Back from the sea.

Islander

Our first ancients were islands.
We were their first children.

They built us
here.

The tall thigh bone
– the I beam

the eye socket
– the lacuna for light

the small cavity near the thigh bone
– also the place for light.

Lacklander
is the word

for those who don't
have land.

We don't have land.
We have the sea.

We islands with our spaces
for the lakes and the rivers.

Eye

Salty lagoon
separated from the sea by bone.

Latitude and longitude dangle thin feet
in your brackish water.

The word

after Dinah Hawken

Still, and after all this

we call light
light.

And especially when it goes out,
we call it.

Light.

Even though it's not the beginning of the world anymore

Ancient light still comes lapping in from space
Making a place in which vision is possible

An opening in the wall for the admission of light
An opening in the wail for the admission of light
An opening in the wall for the obstruction of fear

In which an opening
You can hardly bear to

Gannets nest in there
And paint the dark walls

Bonefire

A hillside of houses leave

Steeped in old weather the wooden houses
remember their bird-selves and unfold
barely-jointed wings.

Door frames spring apart into
the steeple shape of breastbones

there is a woody straining
then the clatter of press and lift
and dozens of pairs of outstretched
wings slow-beat.

The mainland shuffles back.
The sea floods underneath.

Splinters feather frost-burr
along leeched beams.

People curl inside
the bones that keep them
that will not keep them long.

Bonefire

The mainland is rendered down
silvers and is gone.

My heart is green and raw – a pea not a heart –
front to the fire back to the wind.

The groan of stone on stone unsettles
me as I unsettle them.

A passing orca's generator heart opens
and closes the island like a door.

Behind me green bush is a swaying glossary
I could lose myself in –

leaf bird tree feather bone
rock ponga pebble koru stone

bone-fire oil-lamp song
heart gale right whale wrong

Inside the island

It's no use turning my head aside now – this is what I wanted
to be inside the island, inside its green puzzle;

so this empty house with its stroke victim slump
is history – press in

the brown-edged rhododendrons with their sharp, glossy leaves
the freesias so sweet in the half-shade they suggest their own decay

press them in. Make a daybook of yesterday. Note how the island
absorbs the house, the garden, into its dark, vegetable centre.

But I want to say *is this your freedom?*
And why would you live here? Would you live here?

And how would you make differences in the repeating days?
And who would chose loneliness?

It didn't look like this from the mainland.
Don't you think? It didn't look like this?

Interislander

In the ferry's café a man with a heart attack wouldn't release the route guide
for the Kepler Track, which in his fist went damp, land-shaped;
    a contour-map.

The ferry slowed, then turned a circle so hard it seemed to be turning on us,
its passengers, so when the captain announced we were returning we
    already knew –

we had felt the deep spiralling of water beneath –
we understood that we were going back.

Those of us not so obviously dying walked quickly away from the café,
each footstep's pressure on the deck, its sound – the slap

or clack – bearing no relation
to the man who clutched and grimaced on the floor.

We didn't stop walking until far enough away (at the bow, the stern)
to think death a kind of disability we luckily, luckily didn't have.

But the helix twist beneath us wouldn't let go; it compromised
our walking, made a flutter in our eyes.

Our talk lifted like gulls above our bodies at the railings
with their scattered surface rhythms from the ancient deep-red gorges.

The Desert Road

Mount Ruapehu breaches clouds –
a whale arrested in a dive
fluke still planted in the earth.

Driving back through tussock
barnacles of shining white
and the high ice-creaking calls locate us.

Wet banks move, striated, through slow day-lights
shunt time, whole eras, ahead and behind
carry small architecture on great backs.

We cut across this old wake, our father,
the suspension shakes and shakes
we can't make the corners fast.

It gets dark and the languages come out
in constellations and even though we don't know how
we follow them to familiar places.

Backtofront

My lover and I had been
to the hot baths at Hanmer Springs
– Hanmer in the fold of mountains.
Warm from the inside out,
we drove past a country fair and stopped to
let the outside in because we were so
so in love with everything –
the clamorous vaults of winter air
our bird lungs warm
the warmth between our legs
(it seemed we had released our past
our dead) we were
greedy for the fair brewing among the black-
beech and rimu.

We hopped out
pushed the cold doors shut with the tips of our
fingers and walked into
a rack of pigs on hooks – close-up bristling coat,
black-blood at the nose,
fat silver crooks between tendon and bone,
breeze whistling through the cleft of skyward hooves –

this was the corridor in – there was more to come.
Boys and girls in swannies and gumboots
doing an obstacle course, their parents
on the side-lines yelling blunt motivations.
Each child's neck bound
by the front legs of a piglet
dead – strapped to their backs.

The children staggered with their burdens
like old men and old women,
the piglet heads tipped back and juddering,
and when they dropped to crawl under a pole
the dead face thumped forward onto their neck, or head
or shoulder. A thump, a thump, *a tap*.

And when they climbed over the last hay bale
and reached the end the parents called
'Now go back!' and my lover laughed.

At the car the sky had fallen messily
into the valleys,
my hand was clumsy, cold and blue,
I pulled at the door handle then let it slip
bent my fingernail right back.
Belted in and facing out, your hand
beating time on my thigh
to some infernal inner song you knew
you'd lost me somewhere back between
the pigs and kids.
You just felt something in me
and between us fade.
We followed the thin road down the mountain
until the mountain too gave way
to distance, growing shapely and distinct
in the rear vision mirror.

New Feats of Horsemanship

I (young self) and lover walked down Bowen Street
in Wellington, the southerly curled
around the harbour, just beginning
to get up. We weren't
after or before that day's history, we were
the fabric through which
the southerly tore
the way one is at that age –
against soft carpet or concrete,
or flattened against a telephone pole: *Ahh*
Ahh, Ahh

Then later I learned about echoes
and etymology.

Still, some language doesn't need to be
grafted from another tree, it's in us
to yell *Fuck* to the street
or to call back, leaning from our windows,
Ahh, Ahh, Ahh

I don't know when my English began.
Possibly when the bush was cleared
and my lying down branches
went silent. And the branches went silent.

So then, someone had to call memory
in from the wild. *Ahh* we went, and
Fuck down the empty street – mud like slime,
someone on the piano and gold on the lips
through which the southerly tore. *Ahh*
A flying fuck first meant sex on horseback –

it's written in an 1800 broadside ballad.
We were children who broke hearts
by leaving home or by not leaving home.
We went on breaking and breaking into hearts,
fucking on the broad back of what moves us.
Calling to each torn other in creature-language –

Ahh, Ahh, Ahh
Ahh, Ahh, Ahh
Ahh, Ahh, Ahh

Lineage

I was nine months pregnant, and waiting, when the man in the
Taranaki airport shop snapped *this isn't a library you know*,

and when I turned my great belly full of fingernails and teeth-in-bud
towards him he asked (hotly) if I was *actually* going to *buy* anything.

The baby made exclamation marks with its soft bones,
glared with its wide open eyes – two Os. *No* I said *I won't buy*

my news from you. Above the town, Mount Taranaki blazed red and then
in the quick cold dusk the plane with my parents in, touched down.

That night the child swung from its treehouse to the tree
and climbed through me to my mother's hands and with its

persimmon tongue brought us stories (both good and terrible)
from this world, and the other one.

The remembered evenings

On the old-style TV
a hummingbird quivers –

a million wingbeats per minute.

Inside your chest
the heart's murmur.

A slow flight across the living room wall.

Tick and hum.
A million-trillion beats per m.

Your heart is one expanse of strings
stretched tight across another.

Tick and hum.
Mild surprise.

Tick
hum. On the TV screen
a trillion trillion bpm

just to hover over a flower.

Leaving Wellington

At dawn I caught a taxi to the airport
and saw first light ignite the hillside houses –
and I thought about how still life artists deepen
the surface of their objects with a bloom
that, without saying, evokes a place with people
the way those rising houses implied rooms
to escape the wind, to circle in, to slacken.

The plane drops its grey shadow in the sea
and the shadow pulls back slightly, like an anchor.

Hours go by and elements still gather.
Each day my waking children, just by naming
assembled all the solid things of world:
the bath, stove, chair, the bed, the window,
the shoe, the dinosaur, the door, the wall.
Then in a kind of via negativa
they composed two empty rooms by leaving home.

I said it was an anchor but it's not.
It's a shadow roughly like a kiss.

Some say that planes are dead and airless spaces.
Not dead, I think, but deep, with lights on exits.
We tilt into thin air, that fragile outscape,
we press our bulk against some scrubby cloud,
as though against our mother's side for safety
as though there is a place for us to hide.

Then this second dawn that rises all around me –
this long, slow morning with its double bloom –
evokes those first, wild moments of strange waking
from the dream's uncanny tilt to steady form.

Inside the plane we turned to face our windows,
we clutch of hatchlings straining from our nests.
The ground like an oiled platform lifts to meet us
and we fumble with warm buckles on our laps.

We stand in aisles with fists around our baggage.
We stand in isles with wintered earth behind.
We stand like grass in summer, barely moving,

yet like an ear the earth hears news of us.

Inside our cells the numbers of our children.
Inside this surface life, a living room.

Yellow feathers

I'd been teaching in Melbourne's old
Infectious Diseases Hospital –
we'd been talking about voice
for four hours.
I went to the Aids Memorial Garden
to unwind, and that's where
I saw the sign:
Men Doing Tree Work.
From the white gum's
vast spreading branches
thick ropes hung, almost
touching the ground.
Up among the limbs
where the hanging ropes began
crouched men
in high-vis vests
yellow, orange, green –
quite still, barely flickering
up there in the eucalypt haze.
Below the men
the heavy ropes glowed
deep and still in pooled sunlight.
I also stood still,
my hands hanging.
    All of us as if
        and the tree trailing its ropes
like a hot air balloon
    except

Then later, on the train, going home,
a shabby man sat beside me.
Perched on his arm
a sulphur crested cockatoo,
and without words, just with a gesture
he had the bird unfold
one wing to show the sweep
of yellow feathers underneath.
Then he said, you can touch him.
He won't hurt you.
Touch him here.
Like this.

Saturday night in bed

My window open, bar the sieve
of insect netting. A frayed dark
that cools the room, lifts the sound
of voices from All Nations Park.
Shouting. Running. Staggered breath.
Hearts like shuddering compass needles.
Shrieks. A kazoo. People finding each other.

Last night a hectic dream of hares –
muddy, thudding, hurtling things,
who suddenly stopped and then one put
a wide grey paw on another.
Their stopping was complex, considered,
human – they gauged each other.
Then, creaturely in their collective purpose,
they took off on huge grey haunches
with thumps that seemed to move right through me.
I woke up with them in my chest.

I push the little window wider,
tilt the frame to its wildest angle,
let in more night, the sudden screams,
the dogs, the stoned, the stink of bats,
the uncorked fizz, the damned kazoo
and other brilliant passing freedoms.

In All Nations Park

The red breasts of rosellas
make small deep fires in the gumtree.

The dusty-pink bellies of galahs
make clouds of warm ash in the gumtree.

I stand under the tree that flickers with flame.
I understand the tree that shivers with ash.

The ash is still pink,
it has not finished carrying the fire.

In each bird-body, ghost gums
unfold into the hinterland.

It is in our nature
to bear each other.

We think we stand apart
in our burning and transforming.

That nothing could be further.

But the friction of our touching makes tenderness.
It rises like blister-skin, lit from within.

Toowoomba

A pressed tin ceiling
painted a yellowish cream
pings in forty-degree heat.

Two American bulldogs
in surrealistic arrangement
melt into each other on the wrap-around porch.

Sash windows
hang on weathered walls.
The watered-down light comes in, like a buyer.

Someone's daughter (mine)
walks across a long-parched lawn with an imprint of flowers.
She pats the horse   she loves

the big old house   I have swum into   the light
bleaches our hair   she makes us lapsang souchong tea so strong
she makes possums drum the singing roof.

Wild

All that's left that's wild
is in my head –
the shaking canopy under a bone-bright sky –
understory under that
then forest floor soft like a kneeling-pillow
for prayers tapestried with kōwhai and tūī.

A storm is one violet petal
in a puddle, the stain of it
juddering across skies. No self sees it or sees
the sun slide from leaf to branch to leaf
or says *dappled, stippled, freckled.*
Just the space for light dropping through me

as imagined in the deepest most inviolate
(unhurt, virgin) wild part of me.

Return to Islay

Distillery

After twenty-seven years the glass
contains glacier and winter rains,
the endless ploughings of our head-
down big-shouldered moon,
the peasant's body deep in the peat,
deeper still, the grains in his gut.

Yava, bere, jt, šma, akiti, barley

In the wet transfer of barley to whisky,
or the dry transfer of barley to bread,
is history. Old grains from earthly cracks
stirring up weather. Stirring up weather
right here right now in my head.

Bere

body-like

Roland shows me the heart they made stone
by stone from the ruins
long after the barn had dropped
down on one knee.

Walking to my B&B, slivers
of the low white houses
peel into the sea
and tilt

in moon-shine.
Once called bere
'body-like'
the barley for the bread.

As if not dead, you duck your head to hear
the whisper-sound of my palms
rubbing together – a drift
of barley flour

for bread. Up lifts the wave
to saturate the peat with salt.
We will be salt-drenched
before we are brackish dry.

On this wondrous cold island
this is what I hold in mind –
you cannot go inland enough
to avoid the salt

and it will dry against you
and it will rise up through the still
and even
through the broken bread.

Salt

I've been thinking about maintenance and continuity,
and my body, its machinery.
At the Kilbride River,
by iron-tinted stone,
a crane's long arm hovers
poised to mimic what humans do
for benediction –
pour water into water
pronounce the valid, valid
the blessèd, blessed.

A kind of benediction before I left.
Dinner at a rambling Breaker Bay house
with the best of Wellington's dramatic coast –
cliffs behind and sea out front –
and the salty clamour and peaty thump of Laphroaig whisky
to toast me off. Because our countries know each other.
We have our glossy bodies of sea,
our bull kelp, our seals, our rough tracks
our ordnance survey maps.
Only the politics are saltier here,
applied to aggravate and clean.

Crane wakes me with a creak,
I look along its arm into the distance
where a copper still gleams and for an instant
I see a woman squatting on her haunches –
a Sheela na gig holding herself open,
delivering the earth taste.
The glass tips at the edge of the universe.

An Tigh Seinnse

a pub in Portnahaven

My hot chocolate comes with its provenance.
The dark-haired waitress
describes how they bring quality African cocoa
into the island – she leans in, points,
see how the brown is almost purple?
Oh yes, the way the best things always edge towards
being something else.

How small this room is and how
dark the interior,
the still, dry air coiled and threaded
through rafters, like sails
and the furniture that little bit
too close together.

She asks
Have you seen a cocoa pod?
I have, I have.
It's this size, like a draw-purse or wee coracle.
You could go to sea in it.
I did. I went to sea in it.
And here I am.

Wherever I am

I am marginal, a guest.
Sorley MacLean writes this
and it sounds true.
Still, doubt's little motor
turns
threatens to catch.
I catch up with a friend
who shares a walk into
shallow russet hills.
We talk about home, Incline into
our conjurings, conjure up
our upbringings – until we run
dry and stop so the ground
can sound – say moorland.
And I want to say *undulating*
but that's us, so up and down,
drumming up memory and rites of passage
over this shifting underlay
of mica schist and limestone.
Salt blows from the coast
into the hinterland.

Moorland Estate
for George and Fiona

I am asked not to photograph
the crouched black castle with its gaping holes,
(the pale stain on a dirty wall
where a famous mirror isn't anymore)
or the trees poking at its borders, the creaking forest
or the sudden bay where seals turn blacklight eyes on us
as they unglaze themselves on rocks.
Some Fiona rescued as orphaned pups –
the dark shape humping along the shore,
the distressed bark into her ear.

Each mild or frozen morning
she still plays her violin for the slick
dark heads that bob between bull kelp and rock.
I try to imagine that sort of continuity,
and fail. Low sun on glossy water and
sometime snow.

I walk behind her back to the house
where in the courtyard peacocks
drag or fan their tails
both twenty-seven years ago, and now.

In the dim living room
light strikes a wooden cross and
the veil of dust across my cup.
Here believing is breathing: Christ,
fairies, the ghost of the Laird –
his kilt spreading and collapsing on George's legs.

It's been twenty-seven years and it's been a day.
A fair-haired child is an adult steampunk fairy now.
Nothing has changed. The orb-eyed baby seal
is in the bath. We look through layers
to find each other. We greet the dead
across a cup of tea. The dead are wearing jeans
and push their sleeves, like us.

Fiona, who is kind, kindly drives me part way home,
and on the way she calls at the doctor for the arthritis in her hands.
The ache.
All those cold dawns and dusks and splashing days.
All those notes and strings and long, slow bows.
The quiver of fish, the turn of a head, the stain of sun on oily sea,
the pock of rain. All those every-days.
The cold.
All the rescue missions and the heavy, dark bodies.
The trembling arc over the bath before you ease
the frightened, muscly creature in.

All the holding in place. This piece of earth.
The crumbling castle.
(Others say *decline* and *terminal* and *shame*.)
George and Fiona are letting the trees grow through it.

Who am I again? Are you lost again?

We're stories telling stories, nothing
      Ricardo Reis/Fernando Pessoa

The slow unspool of glacier
across a winter-tightened land.
A seaweed-brindled reef
grown from an old gas-line.
The morning or the evening
the mourning or the even-ing.
You could be any thing you like
(although, dressed as you are, as a person,
I'd suggest going with that
despite its time-consuming reflections).
Just do me this favour,
stop divvying up past and future
here and not-here
or there'll be no vantage point
that isn't just a trick
of light.

The inbreath

I went further along the road towards Ardbeg
and stopped by another crane
paused and forgotten, arm extended
where it has lifted water from the river's mouth,
water the slipstream from shipping lanes
spiked with oil spiked with rust.

I sat with it and it unsettled me
with its creepy sudden creaks in the northerly –
and yet that stiff reach over water, over time
suggested private beauties I couldn't know – the nights
when that dark arm holds out a bowl of snow.
Then I wondered if, out of wildness,
the teenagers might go there –
bright snow on the inbreath, and on the bottle's lip.

Return

I walked the thin road back,
one slow movement in dusk's animation,
when the sky washed out
exposing the bens splashed with gold light
then washed in again, stained sea-
anemone-red, and this red sky
flickered drawing me in
releasing me beyond Laphroaig Distillery
to Port Ellen where all the white-washed houses
      are birds
             standing on one leg
             at the Bay's gleaming edge.

Standing Places

Standing Places

At the corner store I ask for sticking plasters
and the young man thinks for a moment
then says 'like for *wounds*' with that Scottish forward
press on words, so wound is almost
manifest; it blooms.

Yes wounds I say, relieved we understand each other.
I was steeled for more explanation,
had *scrape* and *scratch* up my sleeve
even, if I must, *Elastoplast*
but luckily wound does it.

He reaches back
across his right shoulder and finds
a pack. I drop a coin into his dark
hand and wonder if his parents
or grandparents sometimes stand
at the end of words
to worry over their version
of *jug, bench, bach, bush, plaster,*
and what strange sibling-word
might lead them home.

There are plasters enough for sixteen wounds.
I tip out four.
One for my son who is learning
how to live alone.
One for my father who is worn out
and misses my mother.
One for the boy in the store with his
generous topple into *wound*. That's three plasters –

and the one I unpeel now to cover and protect
the slantwise cut
caused by changing points of view,
the wounded aspect.

Country

Frolic in your light bones lamb
and I'll negotiate the narrow lane –
call me in (or is it out) to the fields
with your staccato repetitions
into the barley field which
bends like a smirr of rain
across the day.

In Pukerua Bay the rain smirred
although we didn't call it that
and the nor westerly blew for weeks
and the whole beach was grey
and seagulls hunkered all squinty-eyed
and terns lined up along the shore
showing us their neat black backs,
their sharp clenched wings and
the answering clench of my shoulder blades –
long logs shucking water
as they crest, roll, beach

and nobody came.

At home there are whole days
when you couldn't give the holiday baches away –
windows fogged with salt spray
it's cold and the wind blows, blows, blows
the centre out of your bones;
you look out to where waves thump
and the terns have flown
horizons sharpening and tilting in
their eyes, weather turning still
and crisp as they get higher.

At the ash lagoons I see godwits
and I want to cry. No one speaks my
hollow bones or knows
they are a tribe. Godwits
are bird and book and Robin Hyde,
bird and book and Robin Hyde,
no one speaks my knows the
inside out upside down bones of me.

Country is no solution
but I love, I say, the cobbled streets
the stone houses
perched on the far edge of the ploughed field
looking out –
It's like the beach
I call over to myself, in the bones of you
but lonely as fuck on smirry days
and doesn't solve a thing
not a thing, nor will a berry or a lamb, although
perhaps a flooded field could solve loneliness –
when you think of solution as something cleansing
or medicinal distributed in water.

My field

My star field
My braced wire field
My folding field
My new foal field
My hill pasture field
My skullcap field
My furrowed field
My arable field
My water field
My green-wind field
My zinc bucket field
My foot-stomp field
My one-poppy field
My heron field
My dog-bark field
My flap-flap field
My clacking field
My whistle field
My snowline field
My running dog field
My dog-stop field
My step-back field
My star-scatter field
My dog's wet dance
In the green-wind field

Crows in the skylark field

with thanks to Jane McKie

Counting his gold and finding it wanting
the lover who lives in the castle –
our lips – prepares for battle;
curses too radical to repeat, they would blacken
the crows rising from wheat.

*

It would feel like this. A new weight.
Your mouth pressed down.
I lean my forearm across

*

you.
Storm on the way.
The sky inks up, threatening rain,
but the heat soaks in, spilling crows.
    A skylark
hovers over the pale tasselled field.

*

It's all I want to hear
forever. And when it ends abruptly,
it's all I want to hear.
You tell me I'm beautiful,
like a zebra's stripes.
I wear bluebellvine in bands.

*

Sprouting flowers
stalk
the wheat.
We move our green lengths
here.

Pearls

The physicist says the world
is not a world
of things, it is
a world of happenings.
More a kiss than a stone.

The physicist says we swim in time
as though time were an atmosphere
we hold around us
with our bodies.

We are also each a world
of happenings. A kiss
then a stone. Deep in
my son's ear canal are pearls of bone
made by the little irritation of the sea
going in there and in there
while he surfs. The doctor says
they look like pearls
and then goes in himself,
to remove them.
He – my son – just wants a quick recovery,
he just wants to be back in the water.

Time goes slower in the sea
and faster in the mountains.
Physics has taken over
where poetry left off.

Talking about back home

If you touch wild birds it is a marvellous feeling
   Lucian Freud

Years back in a Wellington art school
the man who would be Tilda Swinton's partner
painted a series of vaginas.
Some of the students modelled for him.
I taught creative writing there in studios, skirting the couch,
the daybed, the drapes.

During one exhibition a big vagina hung over the stairwell
and when I walked downstairs I seemed to be being born feet first,
In my boots, clop, clop, clop into
the world.

I have been born into my country many times.
So why did I say *Yes* when I didn't mean it
to a question I didn't believe in –
the peripherality (or not) of islands –
when I was just talking about home?

It left me floundering, swimming over my plate, my knife
my spoon, my wine. Suddenly having nowhere
to return to. The table was so long, so wide.
I long for the fierce grace of Tilda Swinton
who wouldn't say *Yes* instead of *I*
instead of *home*   instead of *born there.*

And the paintings, more accurately, were of vulvas.
They were thresholds. They weren't the living room
or the hallway.

And I am from the radical centre like most people I know.

Muirhouse Library

Hame

Boy walks into the library –
all his energy before
and behind him.
Sees his mother, calls to her something
about going hame.
Home, his mother says. Not hame. Home.
It's funny how his energy falls flat,
no longer haines him.
Home. Like hame. But farther.
His mother's shy help
in the library
shames him. Hurts her.
Strains and tires them.
Help, like hinder halt or hitch.
Like mum and how she holds him.
Holds him.

When Yellow's on the Broom

Scots is on the lips of all the kids, lips dyed blue from the sweeties.
Deid and heid are there, and hame and hoose and dinnae ken, and I wonder
are these barely-making-it places holding the Scots language now?
Or is that romantic?

In New Zealand the yellow gorse that settlers brought in for ornament
spread everywhere and neither grubber nor poison
nor all the PD workers under bare skies can contain it —

I thought about what's left when big wheels seem to crush us,
and how these things are still affordable: outside fires, our mates,
our locality (the places where poverty is shunted, decanted) and our language.

and then, quite recently, we noticed how its spacious, prickly architecture
makes a nursery for natives; the alchemy of regeneration breaking spiked earth,
unfurling inside buttery arches.

I try to shush teenagers raging on 30p energy drinks and the deep sting
of their parents' habits and one girl says *This is Muirhouse doll, we won't be*
quiet. And they won't and everyday we have to ban them and every next
day they're back again and

when the library closes what they've left comes into focus: wrappers, donut
boxes, tipped chairs, a yellowish splat of sick and a fire in the wheelie bin.
Placeholders.

What I saw

I saw
a dipper in and out of a stream
pouring through composition, through song.

I saw
bull kelp on Islay
make a shore like my shore.

I saw where my great aunt stepped out
in her stylish cinched-waist coat,
out of private violence into the frail home of the street.

I saw
the language inside my language –
yolk, shell, nest: a chaos of need, then flight.

Mist

Mist slips through trees, filling all the spaces
like the photo-bombing ghosts
in olden-days photos.

But really days aren't olden.
It's not days balancing their stacked white bones
on the edge of a couch.
Days don't crack and cleave and leave.

People and trees and birds get old
and die and become olden.
Furniture can be new then old.
And our children.
Photos keep getting old
but their ghosts are frozen.

Weather is not weather.
Time does not do.
But the mist surely does
roll in with the mellowing of light
and with the berries
and with the yellow leaves.

Milk

*Heel print in a pile of dung. Fill it with milk so the king will come. Walk
away with the jug, light now, its milky rim tapping against your thigh.*

He who'd been a man, through mad misdeed –
refusing love, refusing change –
was turned into a bird.
Who once was king with subjects, family
and all the kingly trappings, as a bird
sat at the edge of things. Had done for green
summers and bare winters. Thought himself
forgotten. Until now.

He knows it for what it is. An invitation
back into the fold.
This gathered white for him to sip.
His little heart races.

He lands lightly on shit
to drink – instead of sweet rain, or rose-stained dew,
or snowmelt from a stalk (held still
with one twiggy claw) or pewter pearls
on moss, or glisten from the cleft of a rock –
milk.

Sip. The whole kingdom runs through him.
A shudder. He tries to settle
his feathers. Wants back
to raindrops served on a leaf, wants
back to glossy berries, their juice, not
this sweet milk in its savoury dish.

But he can't stop now, and again inclines to drink
and remembers his territory song.
Thinking of his children, his wife, he hops
up the great path towards the castle.
He wants to touch them, feels the branching
twigs of his claws clump and broaden,
he stumbles towards his arms.

Tonight at table they will eat quail inside
woodcock inside partridge inside pheasant. He
wants to be inside his kingdom, his castle, his
children's arms, inside his wife.

He stops. Horse shit or cow shit
his dark plate? He doesn't know. Surely
he should know. By taste? He shudders
and hops, and steps and hesitates;
and who poured it – calling him back? And
to what?
Thinking of his daughter
he looks towards the castle. Feels the unfurling

of one hand and then the other. And his son.
Feels the tack of the cold wind
around his bare shoulders.
He remembers love and its confusions
and then his wife, paler, and his children
taller, run along the path towards him.
Drape a heavy cloak around him. Draw him
inside. Into still, dry air to soothe
his heart's heavy freedoms.

His fool, of course, his fool has called him.

This thing on my wall

is a felt angel
and there's a bell hanging
from its feet
and even though I kind of hate
fake angels I hang it
on my bedroom wall
above the heater and when
I lean there for heat I ring
the bell by mistake because my back
or shoulder touches it and
it seems to startle up
a moment of pause, a kind of suspension
brief as a wingbeat. Call it
cartoon   draft   scale model
call it plastico. The thing that starts
the thing that represents.

I bought the felt angel
for someone else. It was Christmas
and the angel was a kind of joke
with vulnerable attached (the bell) –
a felt thing I didn't send
because of all the ways I don't
and can't seem to.

How the accidental bell shakes things up –
hope and. Oh maybe just that. Hope really,
and stillness. A kind of presence. Two thrushes
on a bare but budding branch
outside my window. Their whipping glances in here
like very old artists who, I've noticed, kind of look around

like birds, quickly and deeply, seeing
beneath the surface to what is veiled –
a bare shoulder inside your shoulder,
a child in black and white across your chest. A burnished sun
rising from your head. All the bodies and compositions that intersect
and breech the borders of your body, what's deep and what's depicted.
The tears on the fold line. The black holes.
The hands in the cracked bowl, making the kind of bread
you love.

Susanna and the Elders

by Artemisia Gentileschi

The Elders will have her
or falsely accuse her.
We see on Susanna's face
that she knows what is coming,
but the fear is untainted
by that knowing. The fear is pure.

There is the layered look of knowing
and there is the stripped back look of fear.

Her eyes are glossy, perhaps with tears
or perhaps with sudden exhaustion.
It is exhausting to know and not know
at the same time.

In the exhibition's many rooms
I find just one face with a similar expression:
Christ's face in Caravaggio's 'The Taking of Christ'
where Judas has kissed
and Christ knows what is to come;
and he has instinctively pulled back
and is terrified, like a boy
going to the gallows.

Susanna's betrayal is more pedestrian.
Less resonant.
After Daniel saves her honour
I imagine her husband and her father
kept a close eye on her. The path
to her private bath in the garden. The entrance.
The liquid light through leaves. Now hardly ever
called up by Susanna.

The monk called you shrill

God, the things men in old-blood
robes will say –
flying across your bared self
low, like a crow across a turned field.

Today, on my walk, I heard a bell.
Distinct. A cow bell ringing
from a small distance,
or a meditation bell
sounding when my eyes are closed.

It went through me like a high tone through glass.
I couldn't see where it came from.

A man in a thick coat waved a metal detector
like a sickle just above the turned earth.
It made an anxious beep
when, below the bared face of the field,
something private was detected.

Earthed

The deer, a fawn,
its four spiked legs gently
to the ground.
Gently, if at all,
and real? I stand there
for long seconds wondering
then move to see it
move, and then
it's gone.
What stays behind is how
two bodies listened to each other
and then I'm sorry
for the idea of spikes and floating
because we listened with noses,
lungs, eyes and ears,
belly, tendon and bone.

Speaking to the otter

It doesn't break the water to emerge, rather
lifts water into otter-shape.

When one makes itself from river in front of me
I say *hello*

– the word formless in air. But oh the need to speak
because I am human, immersed in time, and this creature is fleet.

Different hemispheres

So much is made from thin air,
including daughters and sons.
Also distance.
Mine are thin
thin air away
so it's not realistic
each time there's a break-up or
an operation on surfer's ear
(where bony orbs like pearls
grow along the ear canal)
nor is it possible when the blood moon
bleeds tangerine or there's a power cut
or a storm wrecks a street of houses.
Or earthquakes do. Or something
comes undone. Like when you didn't mean
to unfold and
reveal the heart. When breath when
simple breathing starts
and starts. It's just not viable
when
to come when you
to
listen
it's not
it's hard
because we
for so long

we

and then they flew
and shone and I
wherever I stand in this world –
even at his place
in Brisbane's heat or hers on a wind-torn
hillside in Wellington –
I have to think how to re-enter gravity,

to *put down* my

and
back inside and
then here
we are again.

Bass Rock

Loom: When a ship moves slowly up and down

Primaries flurry the end of the span

Wait

Stop pushing the rock away with your feet
The chicks are chicks yet
The youths are in clubs
Could you wait until they're

Have you seen what they've done in the cave?
Thrown bright paint at silence   At darkness

Even though

Even though it's not the beginning of the world anymore,
neither is it the end.

We have the eye socket.
We have the space for light.

Also sound.
It is important to make sound.
Isn't it? To sound sure?
Because the body is a loom
the words weave through. By which, from silence,
words and names

and also children. The children also
move through the loom. The words and the children.

Although sometimes just the children.
And sometimes just the words.

But see.

There. That spray of feathers.
Those birds soaring, looking for a space to land.

We're all either here, or we've been here
or we're coming.

What tanglement.
What cacophony on the rock. What babble.
What song.

My loves.
My light.
My dearest islanders.